T 18542

The Apsaalooke

(Crow) Nation

by Allison Lassieur

Consultant:
George Reed Jr.
Cultural Affairs Director
Apsaalooke Nation Cultural Affairs Department

Bridgestone Books
an imprint of Capstone Press
Mankato, Minnesota

Bridgestone Books are published by Capstone Press
151 Good Counsel Drive, P.O. Box 669, Mankato, Minnesota 56002
http://www.capstone-press.com

Library of Congress Cataloging-in-Publication Data
Lassieur, Allison.
    The Apsaalooke (Crow) nation/by Allison Lassieur.
    p. cm.—(Native peoples)
    Includes bibliographical references and index.
    Summary: Provides an overview of the past and present lives of the Apsaalooke—or
Crow—peoples, covering their daily life, customs and beliefs, government, and more.
    ISBN 0-7368-1103-6
    1. Crow Indians—Juvenile literature. [1. Crow Indians. 2. Indians of North America—
Great Plains.] I. Title. II. Series.
E99.C92 L37 2002
978.6004'9752—dc21   2001004500

Editorial Credits

Erika Mikkelson, editor; Karen Risch, product planning editor; Timothy Halldin, cover
    and interior layout designer; Heidi Meyer, production designer and interior illustrator;
    Alta Schaffer, photo researcher

Photo Credits

Dennis Sanders and Geri McReynolds, 6, 8, 12, 20
Edward S. Curtis/Montana Historical Society, 14
Marilyn "Angel" Wynn, cover, 10, 16
William Vinje/U.S. Fish and Wildlife Service, 18

1 2 3 4 5 6 07 06 05 04 03 02

Table of Contents

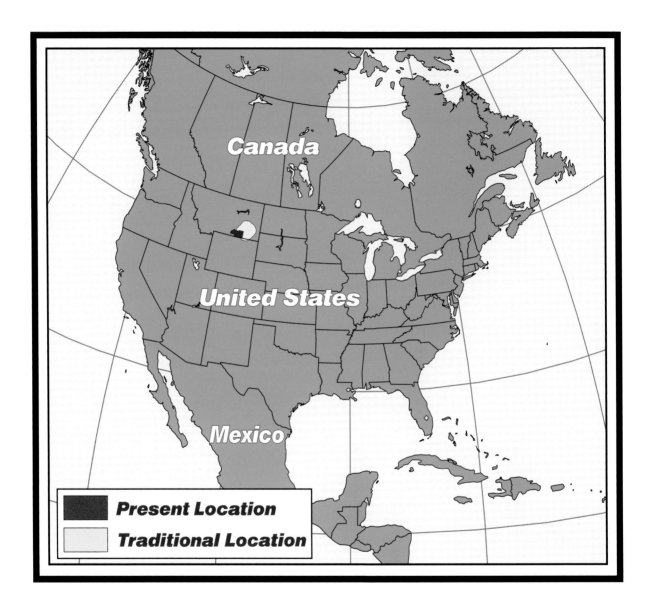

In the past, the Apsaalooke lived along the Yellowstone River in Montana and Wyoming. Today, they live on a reservation in Montana.

Fast Facts

The Apsaalooke (ap-SAH-loh-key) were one of the Great Plains Indian tribes. They were buffalo hunters and horsemen. Today, most Apsaalooke live on a reservation in Montana. They still honor their history. These facts tell about the Apsaalooke people's past.

Name: The Apsaalooke people sometimes are called the Crow. The Crow name was given to them by early explorers.

Homes: The Apsaalooke people lived in large tepees. They built their tepees with lodge poles. They then covered these thick poles with buffalo skins.

Food: The Apsaalooke hunted buffalo. They also ate other animals such as deer and elk. Women gathered vegetables, wild berries, and nuts.

Clothing: The Apsaalooke people made clothing from animal skins. Men wore shirts and leggings made of buffalo, deer, or elk skins. Women wore dresses made of animal skins. Everyone wore moccasins to protect their feet.

Language: The Apsaalooke's language is part of the Siouan language family. Many Plains tribes spoke Siouan languages.

Protecting Their Land

Today, the Bighorn River is part of the Apsaalooke reservation. For years, white people came to the river to fish and hunt. In 1973, the Apsaalooke closed the river. They thought they had the right to protect their lands. The State of Montana said the Apsaalooke could not close the river. In 1981, the U.S. Supreme Court ruled against the tribe. The Apsaalooke were forced to allow people to hunt and fish along the river.

Apsaalooke History

Long ago, a tribe called Gros Ventre lived in the Great Lakes area. About 1600 years ago, a Gros Ventre leader called No Vitals had a vision. It told him to take his people west. Many Gros Ventre people traveled west with No Vitals. They settled near the Bighorn Mountains in Montana and Wyoming. They became the Apsaalooke tribe.

The Apsaalooke divided into four bands. The Mountain Crow moved south of the Elk River. The River Crow group made their homes north of the Elk River. A group called Kicked in the Belly moved west of the Bighorn Mountains. The Beaver Dried Fur band lived south of the Bighorn Mountains.

In the 1800s, white settlers came to Apsaalooke lands. At first, the Apsaalooke were friendly with the settlers. But the settlers killed many animals. The settlers also brought diseases. Many Apsaalooke died. By 1880, the Apsaalooke lived on a reservation in Montana.

The Bighorn River runs through the Apsaalooke reservation in Montana.

The Apsaalooke People

Early explorers gave the name "Crow" to the Apsaalooke. Apsaalooke means "children of the large-beaked bird."

Long ago, the Apsaalooke were divided into different clans. Many families were born into each clan. The people of each clan honored and respected one another. Clan members protected each other and helped one another in times of trouble. Today, many people are still members of their traditional clans.

Education always has been important to the Apsaalooke. The Apsaalooke know that education will keep their traditions and culture alive. Children learn the Apsaalooke language in school. The tribe started the Little Big Horn College on their reservation. Many successful people went to Apsaalooke schools. An Apsaalooke named Bill Yellowtail became a Montana state senator.

Apsaalooke children attend traditional celebrations. They sometimes dress in traditional Apsaalooke clothing.

Homes, Food, and Clothing

The Apsaalooke lived in tepees. They built tepees out of long lodge poles. Each tepee was made from 21 poles. The poles were about 35 feet (11 meters) long. Buffalo hides covered the tepees. A fireplace was in the center. People slept on beds along the sides of the tepee.

Long ago, the Apsaalooke were farmers. They grew crops such as corn and beans. They began hunting buffalo when they moved to the plains. Women prepared the buffalo meat. They also gathered vegetables, wild berries, and nuts.

Apsaalooke men wore colorful and elaborate clothing. They wore shirts, leggings, belts, and buffalo robes. Clothing for ceremonies was decorated with painted designs or beadwork. Apsaalooke men dressed fancier than the women did. Women wore simple dresses made of skins. Women usually had long hair. But some Apsaalooke women cut their hair when a loved one died.

During Apsaalooke fairs, people often build tepees. These tepees look much like the ones built many years ago.

The Apsaalooke Family

In the past, marriages were arranged by a girl's family members. They decided whom the girl would marry. Apsaalooke girls married at a very young age. A man proposed marriage by giving horses to a girl's family. He might also give meat to his future wife's parents.

A married couple joined the woman's family. All children were born into their mother's clan. The mother's brothers were in charge of telling the boys how to behave and dress. Boys learned to ride horses, hunt, and make weapons. Older girls taught their younger sisters how to behave and dress. Girls also learned how to cook and to prepare buffalo meat.

Today, Apsaalooke relatives still have a special role in a child's life. A child calls each of his or her father's brothers "father." All of a mother's sisters are called "mothers." A child calls his or her mother's brothers "big brothers." Older relatives teach the children about Apsaalooke history and tradition.

Family is important to the Apsaalooke.

Chief Plenty Coups died in 1932. He was the last traditional chief of the Apsaalooke.

Chief Plenty Coups

Plenty Coups (KOOZ) was a famous Apsaalooke chief. He was born in 1848. One day, young Plenty Coups had a powerful vision. In the vision, he saw a huge herd of buffalo. The buffalo then disappeared. Plenty Coups saw an old man sitting beside a spring. The old man was Plenty Coups himself. Finally, Plenty Coups saw a storm destroy a forest.

Plenty Coups told Apsaalooke elders about his vision. They said it meant white people would move onto Apsaalooke land. All the buffalo would be gone. Their lands would be taken away. Plenty Coups' vision came true. By 1880, the Apsaalooke were forced to move onto a reservation.

In 1903, Plenty Coups became Apsaalooke chief. He gave the U.S. government Apsaalooke land. Government officials respected Chief Plenty Coups. In 1921, they asked Plenty Coups to help dedicate the Tomb of the Unknown Soldier. The chief put a warbonnet on the tomb. He then prayed for peace.

Apsaalooke Religion

The Apsaalooke believe First Maker created the world. First Maker communicates to people through their senses of sight, smell, touch, taste, and hearing. First Maker speaks to people through their dreams.

The Apsaalooke believe seven powers exist on Earth. Each power matches the seven openings in a person's head. Apsaalooke believe the head is sacred. They do not touch one another's faces.

Long ago, most Apsaalooke went on fasting quests. A person went into the wilderness for many days. He or she would not eat or drink. Apsaalooke believed a spirit would come to that person in a dream or vision. The spirit gave the person a sacred song or object. The spirit might show the future in a vision.

Today, fasting quests still are important. An Apsaalooke goes into the wilderness to pray. He or she looks for a sign from the spirits. When the person returns home, he or she sits in a sweatlodge with tribal elders. The person talks about his or her experience.

This reconstruction of a traditional Apsaalooke sweatlodge shows the wooden frame. Animal skins covered the sweatlodge frame.

First Maker and the Ducks

The Apsaalooke tell the story of First Maker and the Ducks. This story describes how the Apsaalooke believe the world was created.

Long ago, there was a great flood. First Maker traveled the world. He could not find dry land anywhere. He had to sleep on the waves.

One day, two ducks were in the water. First Maker said to the ducks, "Will you dive under the water and bring up some mud? I will make land from the mud."

The first duck dove into the water. When he came up, his beak was empty. The second duck could not find mud either. The duck said, "You fooled me. You almost killed me."

First Maker said, "No, there was land. I stood on it. It then rained for 100 days and 100 nights. I want you to find that land." The second duck dove again. When he came to the surface, he had a tiny ball of mud in his bill. First Maker made land from this mud.

The duck is an important animal to the Apsaalooke.

Apsaalooke Government

In the past, the Apsaalooke lived in four bands. Many clans were part of one band. A chief led each band. He had to do four things to become chief. He had to lead a successful raid. He had to capture horses from an enemy camp. He had to take a weapon away from a live enemy. Finally, he had to touch an enemy with a special stick called a coup stick.

Many men could earn the right to be a chief. The band usually picked the strongest and most respected man as their chief.

Today, the four bands of Apsaalooke live as one on the reservation. A council governs them. There are four people on the council. They are the chairperson, the vice chairperson, the secretary, and the treasurer. The chairperson is elected by the Apsaalooke people. He or she runs council meetings. The Apsaalooke also have an executive committee. There are 14 members on the committee. They are elected every two years.

The Apsaalooke council members take part in festivals on the reservation.

Hands On: Make a Shield

Apsaalooke warriors used shields as protection in battle. They decorated their shields with colorful designs. Each family had a special design. Apsaalooke families placed their shields in front of their tepees. The shields were signs that told everyone which family lived in that tepee.

What You Need

Markers, paints, or crayons
A large piece of poster board or cardboard
Scissors
Masking tape

What You Do

1. Draw a large circle on the poster board or cardboard. Cut out the circle.
2. Cut a strip of poster board for the handle of the shield. The strip should be about 4 inches (10 centimeters) longer than the width of your palm.
3. Think of a design or picture that represents you. It can be an animal, an object, or a colorful picture.
4. Decorate the shield with your design.
5. Tape the strip of cardboard to the back of the shield for a handle. Display the shield for others to see.

Words to Know

ceremony (SER-eh-moh-nee)—formal actions, words, or music that honor a person, an event, or a higher being

council (KOUN-suhl)—a group of leaders chosen to look after the interests of a community

coup (KOO)—an act of great bravery

dedicate (DED-uh-kate)—to show thanks or appreciation to someone or something

raid (RAYD)—a sudden, surprise attack on a place

religion (ri-LIJ-uhn)—a set of spiritual beliefs people follow

reservation (rez-er-VAY-shun)—land set aside for use by American Indians

sweatlodge (SWET-LOJ)—a hut heated by steam from water poured over hot stones

tepee (TEE-pee)—a cone-shaped tent made of animal skins and lodge poles

tradition (truh-DISH-uhn)—a custom, idea, or belief that is passed on to younger people by older relatives or tribe members

warbonnet (WOR-BON-it)—an American Indian headdress with feathers extending down the back

Read More

Kavasch, E. Barrie. *Crow Children and Elders Talk Together.* The Library of Intergenerational Learning: Native Americans. New York: PowerKids Press, 1999.

Tarbescu, Edith. *The Crow.* Watts Library. New York: Franklin Watts, 2000.

Useful Addresses

Crow Tribal Council
P.O. Box 159
Crow Agency, MT 59022

Plenty Coups State Park
P.O. Box 100
Pryor, MT 59066

Internet Sites

Apsaalooke (Crow) Scouts—Little Bighorn Battlefield
http://www.nps.gov/libi/apsaloo.html
Chief Plenty Coups Museum State Park Electronic Field Trip
http://www.plentycoups.org/educate/home.html
Crow Tribal Council
http://tlc.wtp.net/crow.htm

Index